Hacking

*The Essential Hacking Playbook for Beginners, Everything
You need to know before you Start hacking*

Introduction

I want to thank you and congratulate you for downloading the book, *"Hacking : The Essential Hacking Playbook for Beginners, Everything You Need to Know before You Start hacking"*.

This book contains proven steps and strategies on how to prepare yourself to become a hacker. This book effectively introduces you to the world of hacking—the various nooks and crannies, loops and holes.

With this book, will you be prepared for the complex steps hackers usually undertake in order to find security exploits and use it to breach the system. This book effectively deals with the steps you could take *before* attempting to learn hacking in order for you to easily absorb hacking concepts as you learn how to hack. There are also suggestions on how to prepare yourself and gather the resources needed to start hacking. Once you complete this book, then you are finally ready to learn hacking.

Finally, this book deals with developing responsible hacking and skills and attitudes necessary for you to become a successful and useful hacker.

Thanks again for downloading this book, I hope you enjoy it!

TABLE OF CONTENTS

Chapter 1 – Hacking Defined

On September 17, 1993, Rick Dees, the disk jockey of KIIS-FM, a radio station based in Los Angeles, announced the start of their *Win a Porche by Friday* contest in which the 102nd caller every Friday could win one of eight $50,000 Porche. Everyone was glued to their phones. The moment the contest started, all of 25 phone lines of the said radio station rang like hell. The promotional director of the station was counting the call. Somewhere around Los Angeles, someone else was counting the calls, too. Just after the 101st call was placed, all the phone lines of the said station was unable to receive calls from every number except the one from a caller named Michael B. Peters. He dialed the numbers calmly, placed the 102nd call and won the first Porche 944 S2. For the high-school dropout, Kevin Poulsen who was 24 years old then, hacking the station's phone lines and winning the Porche afterwards were no more than a child's play.

Networks of communication might have afforded us all the luxuries of instant and immediate communication. It has made the task of sending and distributing information to a group of people, large or small, across vast distances, easier. We have depended upon it for years with the general and prevalent notion that it can only bring about benefits. Because of our lack of understanding about these complex networks and the mechanism behind their operation, we have grown complacent and believed that nothing bad will happen to us or to our businesses—until an intelligently planned and skillfully executed fraud and thievery such as this happen to us.

What is hacking?

Hacking is an intrusive action based upon the act of finding and exploiting the inherent weaknesses of a computer system (either in their hardware of software structure) and/or the computer network with the primary goal of manipulating the victim's computer and/or network and gaining unrestrained access to the information contained therein.

Hackers are not omniscient creatures of the technological world and cannot perform anything they wish to do. They are bound by certain rules of computing—an area of discipline built upon stacks of programmed rules.

The computing technology, particularly the software (programming) aspects, are new fields of study that we, humans, have never fully mastered, yet, and is beginning to learn and understand how to make it perfect. Because of this, certain flaws in the programming, such that which could allow people from the outside to gain access, are inevitable parts of these technologies. This is where hackers take their strength. They explore and look for these kinds of faults and holes in the network security or in the built-in security modules of a system and exploit them to their benefits.

History of Hacking

The first account of hacking did not happen with computers but with telephone networks. To route calls over long distances, phone companies devised a system of tones (called dial tones). Using a handset and a device used for generating tones called the *blue box*, a phreak (or a phone freak, a term coined for people who break phone networks before computers) could place calls from anywhere in the world. Because of the desire to place calls anywhere without paying for it, people began reverse engineering these tones as soon as they learned about it.

Michael Bruce Sterling, a notable cyberpunk writer, attributes this earliest account of hacking to Yippies or the members of YIP (Youth International Party), who published Technological Asssitance Program (TAP) newsletter aimed at disseminating phreaking techniques to people. People who learned that phone networks can be breached through this technique have begun the culture of belief that all networks must have an inherent weakness in them that can be exploited— these groups of people and the people that followed them and adapted this belief, became what we know years after as hackers.

The history of hacking, though, can be traced as far back to 1903 when Nevil Maskelyne, an inventor, embarrassed John Fleming during his public demonstration of a supposedly secure telegraphy technology. Maskelyne disrupted the presentation by intercepting the communication that is being attempted on the demonstration and sent, instead, an insulting message via Morse code through the projector of the auditorium.

Chapter 2 – Being a Hacker

The objective of hacking varies from minor ones such as gaining access to your own computer after you have forgotten the password to gaining access to another person's computer for malicious intent such as gain access and steal their information (i.e. name, credit card account, passwords, etc.,).

The effects of hacking are devastating. Once a person gains access to a computer, to a network, to an online account or to a website, they can alter the security information in order to restrict your access to these. After doing this, they are then free to do whatever they wish to without you having the power to do anything about it. They can withdraw and transfer money from your account, download and even destroy confidential files and information, gain access to your social media account and to the messages in your inbox, and so on. The possibilities are virtually endless.

Why do people hack?

You may be reading this book because you want to learn how to hack in order to have access to a network or a computer. Reading this book and learning the basics of hacking afford you not only this knowledge but also the capability to detect and prevent attacks against you or your network. You can use the information herein to protect yourself from any methods of hacking.

People learn hacking, in general due to various reasons. Among those are:

- **For fun.** Certain group of people gain satisfaction from cracking or unlocking an encryption. They find the task of breaching securities challenging and get hype from it. In an interview with a teen hacker who breached NASAs network reveals that the hacker did the act because of a power trip—the desire to prove that he was better than the security of one of the most reputable agencies (and systems) in the country without having an actual interest in their information. On certain levels, however, some hackers do not just end with mere hacking the system—they leave malicious software and plant viruses to the victims' system either to damage them or to provide them access to those machines the next time they attempt to hack them again.
- **For personal (and criminal gain).** One of the most dangerous of the hacker's intent is to damage not only the system but the person's reputation as well. Hackers can gain access to an account, steal the information therein, and defraud the owner of the computer or the account. Another group of hackers have now sprung—those who hack a system to have it returned to the owner in the end in exchange for a ransom. These hackers are very patient and follow a carefully formed plan over a long period of time. When their victims system, website or account has already become important, they hack the accounts and have the

victims pay a certain amount to have it returned. Some even resort to actually stealing an amount or placing a purchase using the victim's account. Large-scale hackers target larger companies for lager gains such as the famous Russian hackers who purportedly gained access to various companies all over the world and acquired over a billion usernames and passwords from more than 400,000 sites on the net.

- **To make a statement.** Some activists resort to hacking systems or websites of governments with the intent of halting their operations and services and turning down their websites to make a point and for the government to turn its ears to them. Activists that resort to hacking to have their points heard are sometimes referred hacktivists. One famous instance of hacktivism happened in 2010 when a group of hacktivist took down websites of financial-services companies after they stop donating to WikiLeaks campaign.

When China and the Philippines had a rift, certain groups of Chinese hackers hacked various websites of the Philippines to make a statement and replaced them with banners informing people that the website was hacked by Chinese people because they have the right to a certain island under dispute by the two countries. In response, a group of hackers purportedly from the University of the Philippines, the foremost state university of the country, hacked several important websites of China informing them that they are more capable of hacking and can provide counterattacks to any cyber-attack they perform against the country. These two groups of hackers are examples of people who hack to make statements.

- **To improve security.** Most hackers, especially those who have decided to revert from the criminal habit of hacking, have dedicated their efforts towards improving security against hacking. It is highly reasonable since, because these people know how to attack a system, they are also the perfect people to protect against these attacks. There are certain companies that employ hackers and offer security-related services to other companies. These hackers try to look for security issues in the client companies' systems and report them or devise and design defensive measures. Some companies, like the Internet titan, Google, hosts annual competitions and invites people to breach their systems in order for them to identify the weak points of their systems. Example of these competitions is the Pwnium held in 2014 by Google, which gave prizes to people who could breach various securities included in the company's new OS (Chrome OS). To some extent, these companies also employ previous hackers to have them create systems or improve the existing systems against common and specialized security threats.

Types of Hackers

Before you take on the journey of a hacker, you need to know first what road you are going to take. There are many types of hacker—each has his own sets of skills to develop and specific tasks to master. These different types of hackers are:

White hat

There are generally two types of hackers in the "hat" category. The first is the white hat that does no considerable harm to the victim and the black hat that is inspired by malicious intent. A white hat hacker, the one you most likely are (or will be) if you pursue hacking, is a hacker who breaches security for reasons that are not malicious. Reasons for white hacking include testing the security system of a machine to institute reforms or repairs in a process called as vulnerability assessment and penetration test. Hackers could perform this job for private reasons or under a contractual agreement. Currently, an organization named as the International Council of Electronic-Commerce Consultants provides classes, certifications and online trainings and courses to those who would like to learn about the area of ethical hacking.

Black hat

Contrary to a white hat hacker, a black hat hacker breaches security to perform a malicious act often for personal gain without regard for committing criminal offense. The usual portrayals of hackers in movies and in mainstream media as people who are adept in breaching security in order to inflict harm to the victim fall into the category of black hat hackers. Their usual job includes modifying, destroying (or deleting) and stealing data of particular interest. They can also render a certain network unusable after being attacked. Often, black hat hackers are referred to as crackers by most programmers because of their ability to decrypt encryption protocols. Crackers are able to decrypt encryptions and keep the vulnerability to themselves from the public and from the manufacturers in order to prevent the creation of patches that would remedy the vulnerability. Once a black hat hacker gains access to a system, they may apply patches, fixes and bugs that would help them regain control over the system and ensure that they have the control over a long period.

Grey hat

Grey hat hackers are, perhaps, the most number of hackers out there. As the name suggests, grey hat hackers are both black hat and white hat hackers in the sense that they either inflict harm to the host system or help it improve its system by breaching its security and testing for vulnerabilities. Grey hat hackers often intrude a system, explore its vulnerabilities, and inform the owner of the system about its existence (without being fully detailed about it). They may offer a fee to correct them afterwards. On a darker side, they may also publish it online to inform the public about the vulnerability and the existing of such vulnerability in similar systems without the owner knowing it. Because grey hat hackers tend to breach security without the authorization of the owner, their activities are still considered illegal.

Elite hacker

Of all types of hackers, the most skilled is referred to as the elite hacker. He could be a black, white or grey hacker but with an exceptionally strong hacking skills. He could find and discover exploits to a new system and existing exploits for difficult-to-breach systems are shared among a community of these hackers. They have members and are respected among their groups for their skills.

Script kiddie

There are those who try to hack without actually having the skills to do it. To perform hacking, they run scripts or program for hacking that are coded by hackers. When these scripts or programs are hacked, they perform the routines or the actions necessary for hacking. The limit of script hacking, however, is that there may be alterations or unexpected issues that could render the script useless at some point. Those unskilled hacker-wannabes that use scripts for their pathetic activities are called script kiddies.

Neophyte

Often referred to with the jargon *noob* or *newbie*, a neophyte is someone new to the world of hacking (and, in a much broader sense, phreaking). They are beginning to explore the art of hacking by performing minor hacks or reading reference materials and watching tutorial videos. They do not have experience hacking yet and do not have sufficient knowledge. Overtime, if they become patient and diligent enough, they can become one of the most respected elite hackers.

Blue hat

Hackers employed in security consulting firms, which have the primary job of finding exploits in a system and giving recommendations or providing fixes for them are called blue hat hackers.

Hacktivist

Hacker-activists who uses technology in order for their messages to reach the public are called hacktivists. Most of them are really skilled hackers who can penetrate securities, enter and manipulate a website or compromise an online account just to have their messages heard or read. There are two forms of hacktivists: those who deface websites and do denial-of-service attacks known as cyberterrorists, those that reveal secret information or decrypted information to the public. These groups of hacktivists believe, as the name suggests, that information, especially those who have great impact on the lives of the many should be shared to all.

Chapter 3 – Becoming a Hacker

So you have finally come to a point where the art of hacking will be revealed. If you are a neophyte and have no prior knowledge about how hacking is done, this chapter is for you.

Hacking, however complex it may sound and seem elaborate the steps are, can be brought down into multiple basic steps that can be learned and mastered. You only need to have the right materials and software, the right attitude, the training and dedication required, and the patience. The first steps, as with any other endeavor, is the most difficult. Once you get past it, however, the road ahead will be literarily littered with flowers. You will be brought down a learning path where every new hacking knowledge becomes interesting because you have already understood the basics.

What you will need

In order to start hacking, you need the following:

- **Unix and the ability to operate it.** Although we rarely hear about it, almost all software structures are built upon it. The Internet, for example, runs on Unix. You can become an Internet savvy without even meeting Unix but you cannot become a hacker if you do not know what Unix is, what it does and how to operate it.

  A version of Unix called Linux can be installed alongside Microsoft in a multi-boot system or a system that runs multiple operating systems. Other versions of Unix have known compatibility issues and must be installed alone on the system. If you are running Microsoft and would like to learn hacking with Unix, you must download a version of Linux and install it in your system first.

  The most popular Linux operating system is Ubuntu, which is Debian-based and is also open-source. You can download Ubunto via their website (www.ubuntu.com) and install it to your system via installation options available for Ubuntu. If you do not want to install another operating system alongside your existing operating system, you can run Linux from a disk called a live CD which allows you to boot up to the operating system without modifying your hard drive or messing up with its files. The primary reason why you have to learn hacking with Unix (or Linux) is that this operating system is non-restrictive. There are other operating systems out there like the Microsoft Windows and some closed-source ones. Learning hacking with these operating systems, however, is like trying to explore a field while caged—you are restricted to a small space and can't perform most (usually advanced) functions like what you can do with Linux.

- **HTML.** You can't learn to hack without knowledge about how to write in HyperText Markup Language (HTML). Everything about a website—its design, its behavior and the media it contains—are all ruled and defined by the said language. To have a knowledge of how HTML looks like, you can open your favorite browser (e.g. Google Chrome, Mozilla Firefox, etc.,) and view its page source. Try to dedicate time and energy in learning HTML. You don't need to master it. All you need to do is to have knowledge about how to write it at first. Gradually build up your skill as you learn hacking as well.
- **Programming in various languages.** Computer programs and the software structure that runs them are all defined by the instructions written through a programming language. Programming languages are like bridges to how we think and how machines operate. They translate our ideas into machine behaviors that could result to what we like machines to do. Your level as a hacker will largely depend on your ability to program. Try to learn a language or two and dedicate time to gaining mastery over them. No discipline is easily mastered without effort, particularly areas as complex as programming. The most practical language to learn if you are a beginning programmer is python. It is well documented, it has clean structure and design and is easy to learn. Though it is one of the easiest to learn (and to toy around) python is one hell of a powerful language able to perform tasks and adapt to various formats. Eventually, you will have to learn to program in C, the language in which Unix is built upon, and gradually move up to more advanced C-related languages such as C++. If you have already mastered (or gained sufficient knowledge) about C, learning C++ will be easier.

The Hacker's Discipline

Hackers, as you have already suspected, are not ordinary people with ordinary thinking capability and ordinary skills. They are rare and highly skilled because of a set of attitude they all share (without them even being aware of it). If you would like to be one successful hacker, you need to adapt these attitudes and form a hacker's discipline. Overtime, if you strictly adhere to it, you will become a powerful and skillful hacker who has a great potential to be an elite hacker. Here are the attributes of a hacker:

- **Are highly creative.** Creativity, experts say, is one of the most apparent manifestations of genius. Geniuses are highly creative by nature. That does not mean, however, that those who are not born naturally genius in the craft of hacking must never endeavor to improve their skills. The trick is to develop creativity within you. Creativity allows you to be flexible and be versatile in dealing with situations and in looking for references. Creativity also boosts fun and interest. Read novels (especially about hacking), watch movies, listen to music, draw, etc. Whatever gets your creative juice flowing, do it. This will get your mind to grow more and make the boundaries of your thinking expand further.

- **Develop an interest in problem and riddle solving.** Hackers are highly analytic and have an innate passion for solving puzzles (and cracking codes). This very ability allows them to find vulnerabilities in systems and to decrypt even the most difficult encryptions in securities. If you do not initially love puzzles and riddles (or any game or activity that engages your problem-solving skills), you can try to build up your interest by playing simple computer puzzle games. You can also engage in the computer versions of conventional games that require problem solving such as chess, crossword puzzles, and even math problems. Most of what hackers do is cracking codes to force an entry. If you do not develop an interest to solving problems, chances are, you will have difficulty building your hacking skills.
- **Fight authority.** The human mind has the habit of falling victim to the controlling and restrictive effects of authorities. Free your mind from that mentality. The other people's influence depends upon the degree at which you allow them to affect you. You must understand that nothing must intimidate or bound a hacker.
- **Be competent.** Do not fall prey to the habit of mediocrity. As with any other discipline or endeavor, pushing yourself past your limits will help you get better. Do not slack off. If you cannot do a thing, do not give up. Try as much as you can to learn a thing or conquer a task. If you just can't, take a break and try again until you crack the thing. Hackers have the habit of being unassailed by any task. They try—often to the point of being obsessive and compulsive—without ever giving up until a thing is fully conquered or learned.

Developing the Right Attitude for Ethical Hacking

Nobody can control your hacking experiences after you have learned hacking except you. The path that you will take in the future largely depends on your choices and your decision. Whether you become a black hat, white hat, or grey hat hacker, the decision is up to you. Be reminded, however, that deliberate and irresponsible actions could harm people or affect their lives. The following steps are guides you could adapt in order to tread the path of ethical hacker.

- **Create and distribute useful open source programs.** Hackers are generally programmers and programmers create software that are *most of the times* useful. You can create software that could perform advanced and useful functions, and you can distribute their codes to fellow hackers and programmers in various community pages and forum sites. This type of software or program is called open source because you distribute the codes (source code) and allow others to access and modify it with the intent of improving its function. There are a number of useful open source programs nowadays ranging from utility programs that help keep a system in tiptop shape and speedy brand-new-like state, editing programs used to modify an audio, a video or an image file, anti-malwares, and even programming languages, compilers and decompilers. Try to think about a certain program in a certain platform of your preference (it is more advisable though to create programs in various platforms, although this could be very tasking and that if you are only planning of making your software open source, others could possibly create various versions of your program for other platforms.

- **Help improve other open-source programs.** Test open-source software published on the net and are benefiting a number of people. Look for its vulnerabilities and help improve it by modifying it, pointing it out to the authors or other programmers or creating the fix yourself. A software in a test phase could either be in alpha or beta-testing phase, and you could be an alpha tester or a beta tester. During this phase, it is understood that the goal for this period is to find as many flaw to the program as possible in order to address them properly in the final release.

- **Publish information that could benefit others.** If you are a responsible hacker and someone who knows the dangers and the trauma of having your system compromised, then you already understand the need to educate the many unsuspecting Internet users about the dangers in their systems and how to protect themselves from it. Try to write tutorials about it and post it online through forum sites, social media sites or through a personal blog. Try to post solutions to various computer or system problems, too, that the common Internet user to follow and perform. You can also post tutorials about various tricks to remove malwares, clean the system, find junks within the hard drive, repair the system and many others.

When all the steps outlined in this chapter have already been taken care of, then you are finally ready to embark the journey towards hacking.

Conclusion

Hackers solve problems and build things, and they believe in freedom and voluntary mutual help. To be accepted as a hacker, you have to behave as though you have this kind of attitude yourself. And to behave as though you have the attitude, you have to really believe the attitude.

But if you think of cultivating hacker attitudes as just a way to gain acceptance in the culture, you'll miss the point. Becoming the kind of person who believes these things is important for *you* — for helping you learn and keeping you motivated. As with all creative arts, the most effective way to become a master is to imitate the mind-set of masters — not just intellectually but emotionally as well.

Or, as the following modern Zen poem has it:

To follow the path:
look to the master,
follow the master,
walk with the master,
see through the master,
become the master.

So, if you want to be a hacker, repeat the following things until you believe them:

Thank you and good luck!